50 NAMES YOU NEED TO KNOW!

WHO'S WHO IN...

OLYMPIC HISTORY

CHARLOTTE GUILLAIN

Published 2008 by
A & C Black Publishers Ltd.
38 Soho Square, London, W1D 3HB
www.acblack.com

Hardback ISBN 978-1-4081-0427-9

Paperback ISBN 978-1-4081-1089-8

This book is produced using paper that is made from wood grown in managed, sustainable forests. It is natural, renewable and recyclable. The logging and manufacturing processes conform to the environmental regulations of the country of origin.

Printed and bound in China by WKT.

All the internet addresses given in this book were correct at the time of going to press. The author and publishers regret any inconvenience caused if addresses have changed or sites have ceased to exist, but can accept no responsibility for any such changes.

Acknowledgements
The publishers would like to thank the following for their kind permission to reproduce their photographs:
Cover image: Neal Preston/CORBIS. Pages: 4 AAAC Ltd; Pierre Puget; 5 Ancient Art & Architecture Collection Ltd; 6 Ancient Art & Architecture Collection Ltd; 7 De Agostini/Getty Images; Ancient Art & Architecture Collection Ltd; 8 S&G/PA Photos; Bettmann/CORBIS; 9 IOC/Olympic Museum collections; Hulton-Deutsch Collection/CORBIS; 10 Bettmann/CORBIS; 11 CORBIS; 12 Bettmann/CORBIS; 13 Bettmann/CORBIS; 14 Bettmann/CORBIS; 15 Bettmann/CORBIS; 16 Universal/TempSport/Corbis; 17 Wally McNanee/CORBIS; 18 Douglas Kirkland/CORBIS; 19 F. Carter Smith/Sygma/Corbis; 20 Reuters/CORBIS; 21 Duomo/CORBIS; 22 Dimitri Iundt/TempSport/Corbis; 23 Reuters/CORBIS; 24 Yves Herman/Reuters/Corbis; 25 Reuters/Corbis; 26 AFP/Getty Images; 27 Reuters/CORBIS; 28 Rune Hellestad/Corbis; 29 Eric Fougere/VIP Images/Corbis; 30 Bob King/Corbis; 31 Toby Melville/Reuters/Corbis; 32 Underwood & Underwood/CORBIS; Bettmann/CORBIS; 33 Bettmann/CORBIS; Marc Francotte/TempSport/Corbis; 34 Bettmann/CORBIS; 35 Bettmann/CORBIS; 36 Bettmann/CORBIS; 37 Getty Images; 38 MICHAEL HANSCHKE/epa/Corbis; 39 Georgios Kefalas/epa/Corbis; 40 DPA/DPA/PA Photos; 41 AP/AP/PA Photos; KATSUMI KASAHARA/AP/PA Photos; 42 Getty Images; AFP/Getty Images; 43 Wigglesworth/Pool/Reuters/Corbis; 44 Bettmann/CORBIS; 45 Bettmann/CORBIS.

Contents

Chionis of Sparta

Chionis of Sparta was an excellent all-round **athlete** and one of the earliest Olympic champions.

Sporting achievements

The Spartan athlete Chionis won an event called the **stade** at the ancient games in 664, 660 and 656 BC. The *stade* was a 192.27 metre **sprint** down a straight track. Chionis won a longer race, called the **diaulos,** at the same games. He also set records in the long jump and **triple jump** in 656 BC.

Find out more

For more information visit:
www.museum.upenn.edu/new/
olympics/olympicintro.shtml

Timeline

The *stade* is the only event at the games

900 BC   **776 BC**   **656 BC**

First recorded Olympic Games held   Chionis of Sparta wins his third Olympic title in the *stade*

Milo of Croton

Milo of Croton was a six-times wrestling champion at the ancient Olympic Games.

Sporting achievements

Milo came from Croton in southern Italy. In 540 BC, he won the boys' wrestling competition. As an adult, he was wrestling champion at five Olympic Games in a row, from 532 to 516 BC. Milo is famous for being a huge man with incredible strength. Many legends were written about him.

Find out more

Find out more about ancient Greece and the early Olympics at:
www.ancientgreece.com

Timeline

The games now include jumping, throwing, wrestling, **chariot** racing, and running in armour.

Phanas of Pellene wins three gold medals at the same games.

648 BC   **516 BC**   **512 BC**

Milo of Croton wins his sixth wrestling title.

4

Theagenes of Thasos

Theagenes of Thasos was a boxer, wrestler, and runner who became two-times Olympic champion.

Early life

Theagenes grew up on the island of Thasos, where his father was a priest. One story tells of the nine-year-old Theagenes stealing a bronze statue and carrying it home. His father made him carry the statue all the way back. Theagenes used this strength when he became an athlete.

What they said about him

66 The total number of crowns that he won was one thousand four hundred. 99

Timeline

Boxing added to the Olympic events

Theagenes wins the boxing title at the Olympic Games

Two-horse chariot racing added to the Olympics

688 BC   648 BC   480 BC   476 BC   408 BC

***Pankration* added to the Olympic events**

Theagenes wins the *pankration* at the Olympic Games

Did you know?

Soldiers in the Greek army were trained to use pankration in battle.

Find out more

The British Museum's site has more about ancient Greece and the early Olympics. www.britishmuseum.org/learning/schools_and_teachers/primary/ancient_greece.aspx

Amazing athlete

As an adult, Theagenes became skilled as a boxer and in the *pankration* event. *Pankration* was a mixture of boxing and wrestling that had few rules. In 480 BC, Theagenes took the Olympic boxing title but was too tired to win the *pankration*. He returned to the games in 476 BC and took the *pankration* title. Theagenes also took part in many running events and was an athlete for around 22 years.

5

Cynisca

Cynisca was the first woman in history to win at the ancient Olympic Games.

What they said about her

66 Agesilaus... persuaded his sister Cynisca to breed chariot horses... 99

Did you know?

In ancient Greece unmarried women could take part in their own sporting events at the Heraea Games.

Find out more

Find out more about the ancient city of Sparta at: www.sikyon.com/Sparta/sparta_eg.html

Find out more about the ancient Olympics at the BBC website: www.bbc.co.uk/schools/ancientgreece/olympia/index.shtml

Early life

Cynisca was a Spartan princess who was born around 440 BC. Sparta was a city in Greece. Unlike the women from most other city-states, Spartan women were encouraged to take part in sports. Cynisca grew up riding and hunting.

Timeline

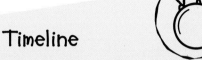

Cynisca born

Cynisca wins again at the Olympics

440 BC　　　　　**396 BC**　　　　　**392 BC**

Cynisca wins first Olympic title

Sporting achievements

Cynisca was the first woman in history to win at the ancient Olympic Games. Not only were women not allowed to take part in the Olympics, but they were not even permitted to watch. However, in the chariot races the prize was awarded to the owner of the horses, rather than the driver. Cynisca had grown up in the world of horse riding and was an expert horse rider herself. She used her knowledge and wealth to train her own horses. In 396 BC, Cynisca won the Olympic chariot race when her horses came first. She repeated her victory in 392 BC.

Leonidas of Rhodes

Leonidas of Rhodes won a total of 12 Olympic titles in three different running events.

Sporting achievements

Leonidas took part in three different running events – the *stade*, the *diaulos*, and the armour race. He won all three races at four Olympic games in a row, from 164 to 152 BC. This makes him one of the greatest champions of all time.

Find out more

Find out about Leonidas at the official website of the Olympic movement: www.olympic.org/uk/games/ancient/athletes_uk.asp

Timeline

Leonidas of Rhodes wins his first three Olympic titles

164 BC

152 BC

Leonidas wins three titles for the fourth time

Melankomas of Karia

Melankomas was a skilled boxer from Karia, in modern-day Turkey.

Sporting achievements

Melankomas won many times without even hitting his opponents. He was very fit, and the other boxers would eventually give up trying to hit him. In 49 BC, he took the Olympic boxing title and he also took part in other events.

Find out more

Find out about Melankomas at the official website of the Olympic movement: www.olympic.org/uk/games/ancient/athletes_uk.asp

Timeline

Olympic Games held in Rome

Roman Emperor Theodosius bans the Olympic Games

80 BC   **49 BC**   **AD 93**

Melankomas of Karia wins the boxing title

James Brendan Connolly

James Brendan Connolly was the first athlete to win a gold medal at the first modern Olympic Games in 1896.

Sporting achievements

The first modern Olympic Games were held in Athens, Greece, in 1896. Only men took part, including an American athlete and student called James Connolly. He won an event called the hop, step, and jump (now known as the triple jump), winning the first gold medal of the modern games.

Timeline

1868	1891	1895	1896	1904	1957
	Sets up an American football team		Wins a gold medal at the first modern Olympic Games		Dies, aged 88
Born in Boston, USA		Studies at Harvard University		Attends the Olympic Games in St. Louis, USA, as a journalist	

Ray Ewry

The American Ray Ewry was one of the most successful Olympians of all time, winning eight gold medals in three consecutive Olympic Games.

Sporting achievements

Ewry recovered from childhood **polio** and went on to win gold in the standing high jump, triple jump, and long jump in Paris in 1900. He repeated this amazing feat in St. Louis in1904 and won two further medals in London in 1908.

Find out more

Find out about Ewry at the official website of the Olympic movement: www.olympic.org/uk/athletes/index_uk.asp

Timeline

1873	1900	1904	1908	1912	1937
Born in Indiana, USA		Defends his three titles successfully in St. Louis		Standing jumps are dropped as Olympic events	
	Wins three gold medals in one day at the Paris Olympics		Wins two more gold medals in London		Dies, aged 64

Helen de Pourtales

Helen, Countess de Pourtales was one of the first female medal winners in the modern Olympics.

Sporting achievements

Helen de Pourtales competed for Switzerland at the 1900 Olympics in Paris, France. She took part in the mixed yachting events, winning gold and silver medals. This made her the first woman to win a medal at the modern Olympics.

Find out more

Find out more about women who have taken part in the Olympics, including de Pourtales at:
www.olympicwomen.co.uk

Timeline

Born in New York, as Helen Barbey

1868

1900

Competes in the Paris Olympics. Her team wins gold and silver medals.

Dies in Geneva, Switzerland, aged 76

1945

Charlotte Cooper

British tennis player Charlotte Cooper was the first female individual Olympic champion.

Sporting achievements

Cooper took part in the 1900 Olympic Games in Paris, France. She won the women's tennis singles to become the first female Olympic gold medallist in an individual event.

Find out more

Find out more about women who have taken part in the Olympics, including Cooper at:
www.olympicwomen.co.uk

Timeline

Born in Ealing, England

Wins gold in the women's tennis singles at the Paris Olympics

Dies, aged 96

1870

1895

1900

1908

1966

Wins the first of five Wimbledon titles

Wins fifth Wimbledon title, aged 37

Jim Thorpe

Jim Thorpe was an all-round athlete who won the **decathlon** and track-and-field **pentathlon** at the 1912 Olympic Games in Stockholm, Sweden.

What he said

❝ I have always liked sport and only played or run races for the fun of the thing. ❞

How did he die?

Thorpe died following a heart attack in his home in Lomita, California.

Early life

Thorpe's family had European and Native American roots, and he was also known as Wa-Tho-Huk, meaning "Bright Path". Thorpe was bullied as a child, but he did well as a member of the college football team.

Timeline

1888	1911	1912	1913	1915	1953
Born in Oklahoma, USA		Wins gold in the decathlon and pentathlon at the Stockholm Olympics		Joins a professional football team	
	Becomes famous in the USA playing college football		Joins a professional baseball team		Dies, aged 64

Find out more

Find out more about Jim Thorpe at his official website:
www.cmgww.com/sports/thorpe

This site includes some information about Thorpe's Native American background.
www.nativeamericans.com/jimthorpe.htm

Sporting achievements

Jim Thorpe went to Stockholm to take part in the 1912 Olympic Games. He represented the United States in the decathlon and the track-and-field pentathlon. Thorpe was an able athlete and easily won both gold medals. His decathlon score remained unbeaten for nearly 20 years. In 1913, Thorpe was stripped of his Olympic titles when it was revealed that he had played professional baseball. Only amateur athletes could compete in the Olympics. Thorpe's medals were eventually reinstated in 1983, exactly 30 years after his death.

Jesse Owens

Jesse Owens was an African–American athlete who stunned the world with his victories at the 1936 Olympic Games.

Early life

Owens was born James Cleveland Owens. His athletic skill was first spotted at school and helped him gain a place at college. Racism was a problem in the United States at the time. As an African-American man, Owens did not have the same opportunities as the white athletes. Even so, Owens broke three world records at one athletics meeting in 1935.

What he said

" For a time, at least, I was the most famous person in the entire world. **"**

Find out more

Find out more about Owens at his official website: www.jesseowens.com

The White House website has a page about Jesse Owens: www.whitehouse.gov/kids/dreamteam/jesseowens.html

Timeline

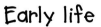

Born in Alabama, USA

Breaks three world records within one hour at the Big Ten athletics meeting

Awarded the Medal of Freedom by US President Gerald Ford

1913 **1933** **1935** **1936** **1976** **1980**

Equals the world record for the 100-yard dash at the National High School Championships

Wins four gold medals and sets three Olympic records in Berlin

Dies, aged 66

Sporting achievements

Owens went to the 1936 Olympic Games in Berlin, Germany, when the **Nazi Party** was in power. German Chancellor Adolf Hitler wanted to use the games to show that the white German "Aryans" were better than the other athletes. Owens destroyed these plans by winning gold medals in the 100m, 200m, long jump, and the 4 x 100m relay. He was the star of the games and became the first American in the history of Olympic track and field to win four gold medals at a single Olympics.

How did he die?

Owens died of lung cancer having smoked a pack of cigarettes a day for 35 years.

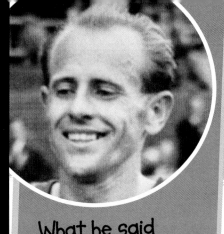

Emil Zátopek

Emil Zátopek was a soldier from Czechoslovakia. He won the 5,000m, 10,000m, and **marathon** at the 1952 Olympics in Helsinki, Finland.

What he said

6699 A runner must run with dreams in his heart, not money in his pocket.

How did he die?

Zátopek died following a stroke. Thousands of people went to his funeral.

Early years

Zátopek was born in Koprivnice, Czechoslovakia, in 1922. When he was 16 years old, he started working in a shoe factory. The factory organized a 1,500m race in 1940. Zátopek came second out of 100 runners.

Timeline

1922	1944	1948	1952	1955	2000

Born in Czechoslovakia

Wins gold in the 10,000m and silver in the 5,000m at the London Olympics

Sets the last two of his world records, for 15 miles and 25,000m

Breaks the Czech records for 2,000, 3,000, and 5,000m

Wins the 5,000m, the 10,000m, and the marathon at the Helsinki Olympics. Sets a new Olympic record in all three events.

Dies, aged 78

Find out more

This site presents a history of running and has a page on Zátopek: www.runningpast.com/emil_zatopek.htm

Find out about Emil Zátopek at the official website of the Olympic movement: www.olympic.org/uk/athletes/index_uk.asp

Sporting achievements

Zátopek was 26 when he went to London to compete in the 1948 Olympic Games. He had very little experience in international competition, but he still won gold in the 10,000m and silver in the 5,000m. Shortly before the 1952 Olympics in Helsinki, Zátopek was ill. He still competed and won the 5,000m, 10,000m, and marathon in the space of eight days. He set new Olympic records in all three events. It was the first time he had ever run a marathon.

Abebe Bikila

Abebe Bikila was the first African athlete to win an Olympic gold medal.

Early life

Bikila was the son of a shepherd in rural Ethiopia. As a young man he joined the army, where he was spotted by a government athletics coach.

What he said

❝I wanted the world to know that my country, Ethiopia, has always won with determination and heroism. **❞**

Timeline

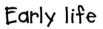

orn in Ethiopia

Wins gold in the marathon at the Tokyo Olympics. He is the first athlete to win the Olympic marathon twice.

Dies, aged 41

| 1932 | 1960 | 1964 | 1969 | 1973 |

Wins gold in the marathon at the Rome Olympics

A car accident leaves him partly paralyzed.

How did he die?

Bikila died when a blood vessel burst in his brain. The injury was related to his car accident.

Find out more

Find out more about Bikila at the official website of the Olympic movement:
www.olympic.org/uk/athletes/index_uk.asp

This site includes a biography of Abebe Bikila:
www.ethiopians.com/abebe_bikila.htm

Sporting achievements

Bikila qualified for the 1960 Olympic team at the last minute because another athlete was injured. There were no running shoes that fitted him so he decided to run the marathon barefoot, the way he had trained. He won the race with a sprint finish. He suffered **appendicitis** days before the 1964 Olympics and had an operation, yet he still took part and won the marathon again, this time wearing shoes. He set a new world record.

Mark Spitz

Mark Spitz is an American swimmer who holds the record for the most gold medals won at a single Olympic Games.

What he said

66 I'm trying to do the best I can. I'm not concerned with tomorrow, but with what goes on today. 99

Did you know?

Not many swimmers have a moustache. Most think it would slow them down.

Early life

Spitz learned to swim in Hawaii as a small child. He began to compete aged six. By the time he was 10, Spitz already held one world record. He continued to train at college where he was nicknamed "Mark the Shark".

Timeline

Born in California, USA

Wins four gold medals at the Maccabiah Games, aged only 15

Made World Swimmer of the Year for the first time after winning five gold medals at the Pan American Games

Wins four medals at the Mexico Olympics

Wins seven gold medals at the Munich Olympics

1950   1965   1967   1968   1972

Sporting achievements

When Spitz went to the 1968 Olympics in Mexico City, he already held 10 world records. Spitz won two gold medals, a silver, and a bronze in Mexico City, but he was disappointed. At the Munich Olympics in 1972, a determined Spitz won an incredible seven gold medals and set four individual world records. Hours after he won his last race, Palestinian **terrorists** murdered 11 Israeli athletes. Spitz is Jewish, so he left Munich quickly for his own safety.

Olga Korbut

Olga Korbut was a gymnast from the former **Soviet Union** who won three gold medals at the Munich Games in 1972.

Early life

Korbut grew up in Belarus, which was then part of the Soviet Union. She began gymnastics aged eight. By the age of 11, Korbut was being coached at a special sports school.

What she said

❝Don't be afraid if things seem difficult in the beginning… The important thing is not to retreat; you have to master yourself.❞

Timeline

Born in Belarus, part of the former Soviet Union

Wins three gold medals and a silver at the Munich Olympics

Wins one gold and one silver medal at the Montreal Olympics

1955   **1969**   **1972**   **1975**   **1976**   **1977**

Competes in her first national championship

Named "Woman of the Year" by the United Nations

Retires from competition and starts to coach

Find out more

The official website of Korbut: www.olgakorbut.com

Find out more about Korbut at the official website of the Olympic movement: www.olympic.org/uk/athletes/index_uk.asp

Sporting achievements

Korbut amazed the crowds at the Olympic Games in Munich. She was the first person to perform three new skilled moves, including the self-titled "Korbut Flip" on the beam. She won three gold medals and a silver medal and changed the way gymnastics was performed for ever. At the Montreal Games in 1976 she was injured, but she still managed to win a gold and a silver medal. She retired from competition a year later.

Did you know?

At school Korbut was the smallest, but she could run faster than all the girls and most of the boys.

Lasse Virén

Virén was a long-distance runner from Finland who won the 5,000m and 10,000m at the Olympics in 1972 and 1976.

What he said

❝Dream barriers look very high until someone climbs them. They are not barriers any more.❞

Did you know?

Virén liked to train in the woods. He said that avoiding the tree roots kept him alert.

Early life

Virén was a police officer in his home town when he first ran in an international competition in 1971. He did not win any races, but he trained hard and qualified for the Olympics the following year. When Virén arrived in Munich, Germany, he was an unknown athlete.

Timeline

Born in Myrskylä, Finland — **1949**

Runs in his first international competition — **1971**

Wins gold in the 5,000m and 10,000m at the Munich Olympics — **1972**

Wins gold in the 5,000m and 10,000m at the Montreal Olympics — **1976**

Comes fifth in the 10,000m at the Moscow Olympics — **1980**

Becomes a member of the Finnish Parliament — **1999**

Find out more

Find out more about Virén at the official website of the Olympic movement:
www.olympic.org/uk/athletes/index_uk.asp

Find out about the stars of Finnish sport at:
virtual.finland.fi/finfo/english/sportsta.html#vire

Sporting achievements

Virén was an outstanding athlete. At the Munich games, he took gold in the 5,000m and 10,000m races. He broke the world record for the 10,000m, even though he fell towards the end of the race. He repeated this amazing long-distance double at the 1976 Montreal Games. In the 5,000m he ran far ahead of all the other runners and stunned spectators with his speed. The very next day, Virén ran in the marathon and came fifth.

Nadia Comaneci

Nadia Comaneci was an outstanding Romanian gymnast who became the first person to score a perfect 10 at the Montreal Games.

Early life

Comaneci started gymnastics at an early age. By the age of six she attended a special gymnastics school. At the European Championships in Norway, when Comaneci was just 13 years old, she won every event apart from the floor, in which she came second.

What she said

"Hard work has made it easy. That is my secret. That is why I win."

Timeline

1961	1970	1975	1976	1980	1981
Born in Onesti, Romania	Becomes the youngest gymnast ever to win the national championships	Wins four gold medals and a silver medal at the European Championships	Wins three gold medals, including the all-around medal at the Montreal Olympics	Wins two gold and two silver medals at the Moscow Olympics	Retires from competition

Did you know?

Comaneci left communist Romania in 1989.

Find out more

Find out more about Comaneci at the official website of the Olympic movement:
www.olympic.org/uk/athletes/index_uk.asp

Sporting achievements

At the 1976 Montreal Games, Comaneci became the first gymnast in Olympic history to be awarded the perfect score of 10. She was given this score seven times during the games and won three gold medals, one silver, and one bronze. At the 1980 Moscow Games, Comaneci took two more gold and two more silver medals. She is widely regarded as the most successful gymnast in Olympic history.

Daley Thompson

Daley Thompson was an extremely popular British athlete who won gold in the decathlon at the 1980 and 1984 Olympics.

What he said

66 I've got the Big G, boys - the Big G! 99

(Referring to his gold medal win in 1984.)

Did you know?

The name "Daley" comes from Thompson's Nigerian name, "Adadele".

Early life

Thompson was born Francis Morgan Thompson to Nigerian and Scottish parents. His all-round athletic ability was first spotted at boarding school, and he competed in his first decathlon at the age of 16.

Timeline

1958	1976	1980	1984	1992
Born in London	Competes in the Montreal Games	Wins gold medal at the Moscow Games	Wins gold at the Los Angeles Games, breaking the world record in the process	Retires after an injury

Sporting achievements

Thompson was already the **Commonwealth** decathlon champion when he won Olympic gold at the Moscow Olympics in 1980. His great opponent was the East German decathlete, Jürgen Hingsen, who was determined to take gold at the Los Angeles Games in 1984. Thompson fell behind in the **discus** event before a fantastic throw put him back in the lead. He won the gold medal again, setting a world record that stood until 1992.

Carl Lewis

Carl Lewis was an American track and field athlete who won a total of nine gold medals at four different Olympic Games.

Early life

Lewis grew up in New Jersey, USA. His parents ran an athletics club for young girls. Lewis joined the club when it was opened up to boys. He started to train and compete in the long jump aged 13.

What he said

❝Get out of the blocks, run your race, stay relaxed. If you run your race, you'll win...❞

Timeline

1961	1984	1988	1992	1996	1997
Born in Alabama, USA	Wins four gold medals at the Los Angeles Olympics	Wins two gold and one silver medal at the Seoul Olympics	Wins two gold medals at the Barcelona Olympics	Wins one gold medal at the Atlanta Olympics	Retires from athletics

Find out more

The official website of Lewis:
www.carllewis.com

Find out more about Lewis at the official website of the Olympic movement:
www.olympic.org/uk/athletes/index_uk.asp

Sporting achievements

At the 1984 Los Angeles Olympics, Lewis won gold in the 100m, 200m, long jump, and 4 x 100m relay, matching the record that Jesse Owens set back in 1936. At the 1988 Seoul Olympics, Lewis won gold in the long jump. His silver medal in the 100m was upgraded to gold after the original winner, Ben Johnson, tested positive for illegal drugs. Lewis continued his run of success at the 1992 Barcelona Games, where he picked up two gold medals. He took his final gold medal for the long jump in the 1996 Atlanta Olympics.

Did you know?

As a baby, Lewis played in the long jump pit at his parents' athletics club.

19

Jackie Joyner-Kersee

Jackie Joyner-Kersee was an American athlete who won gold medals for the **heptathlon** at the 1988 and 1992 Olympics Games,

What she said

66 If a young female sees my dreams and goals come true, they will realize their dreams and goals might also come true. 99

Did you know?

Joyner-Kersee's brother Al was also an Olympic athlete who won a gold medal in the triple jump in 1984.

Early life

Joyner saw a film as a child that inspired her to become an athlete. When she was at college, she played basketball and trained in track and **field events**.

Timeline

1962	1984	1988	1992	1996	2000
Born in Illinois, USA		Wins gold in the heptathlon and long jump at the Seoul Olympics		Wins bronze in the long jump at the Atlanta Olympics	
	Wins silver in the heptathlon at the Los Angeles Olympics		Wins gold in the heptathlon and bronze in the long jump at the Barcelona Olympics		Retires from athletics

Find out more

Find out more about Joyner-Kersee at the official website of the Olympic movement: www.olympic.org/uk/athletes/index_uk.asp

Find out about Joyner-Kersee and other African-American athletes at: www.topblacks.com/sports/jackie-joyner-kersee.htm

Sporting achievements

At the 1984 Los Angeles Olympics, Joyner won a silver medal in the heptathlon. In 1986, Jackie married her coach, Bob Joyner, and became Jackie Joyner-Kersee. By 1988, Joyner-Kersee was by far the world's best heptathlete. She easily won the gold medal at the Seoul Olympics, along with another gold medal for the long jump. Her athletic form continued until 1992, when she took the heptathlon gold in the 1992 Barcelona Olympics. Injury forced her to pull out of the heptathlon in Atlanta in 1996 but her final jump in the long jump won her the bronze medal.

Florence Griffith-Joyner

Florence Griffith-Joyner was an American track athlete who won three gold and one silver medal at the 1988 games in Seoul.

Early life

Griffith was born in Los Angeles. She won her first athletics competition at the age of seven and set many records while at school. Clearly, she was a talented athlete.

What she said

66 When anyone tells me I can't do anything... I'm just not listening any more. 99

Did you know?

At the games, Griffith-Joyner painted three fingernails red, white and blue. She painted the fourth nail gold.

Timeline

Born in Los Angeles, USA		Wins one gold and one silver medal at the World Championships		Dies, aged 38
1959	**1984**	**1987**	**1988**	**1998**
	Wins a silver medal in 200m at the Los Angeles Games		Wins three gold and one silver medal at the Seoul Games	

Find out more

The official website of Griffith-Joyner:
www.florencegriffithjoyner.com

Find out more about Griffith-Joyner at the official website of the Olympic movement:
www.olympic.org/uk/athletes/index_uk.asp

Sporting achievements

Griffith-Joyner's first Olympic appearance was in her home city of Los Angeles in 1984, where she won silver in the 200m. By the time of the Seoul Olympics in 1988, she had developed into an all-round sprinter and won gold in the 100m, 200m, and 4 x 100m relay, as well as a silver medal in the 4 x 400m relay. Florence Griffith-Joyner's nickname was "Flo-Jo". She was famous for her long fingernails and brightly coloured running suits.

Kristin Otto

Kristin Otto was an East German swimmer who won six gold medals at the 1988 Seoul Olympics.

What she said

❝ I know I haven't reached my limits. **❞**

(Otto in the run-up to the 1988 Olympics.)

Did you know?

Today Otto is a TV sports presenter in Germany.

Find out more

Find out what it takes to become an Olympic swimming champion at www.olympic.org/uk/sports/programme/discipline_uk.asp?sportcode=SW

Early life

Otto was born in East Germany. From the age of 11, she trained at a special sports school. She took part in her first World Championships at the age of 16, winning one individual and two team gold medals.

Timeline

1966	1982	1986	1988	1989
Born in Leipzig, East Germany	Wins three gold medals at the World Championships	Wins four gold medals at the World Championships	Wins six gold medals at the Seoul Olympics	Retires from swimming

Sporting achievements

Otto missed the 1984 Olympics in Los Angeles because the East German team **boycotted** the games. However, she dominated the swimming at the 1988 Seoul Olympics, winning six gold medals in individual and relay events. She won in the **freestyle**, butterfly, and backstroke and became the first Olympic swimmer to do so.

Michael Johnson

Michael Johnson was an American sprinter who took the gold medal in the 200m and 400m at the 1996 Atlanta Games.

Early life

Johnson was first spotted as a strong athlete when he was at college. Michael Johnson expected to do well at the 1992 Olympics in Barcelona, but he fell ill and could not run in the individual 200m. He recovered and won a gold medal in the 4 x 400m relay.

What he said

66 If I ran like all the other runners, I would be back there with them. 99

Find out more

Find out more about Johnson at the USA Track and Field website: www.usatf.org/athletes/bios/oldBios/2001/Johnson_Michael.asp

Find out more about Johnson at the official website of the Olympic movement: www.olympic.org/uk/athletes/index_uk.asp

Timeline

Born in Dallas, USA

Wins gold in the 4 x 400m relay at the Barcelona Olympics

Wins gold in the 200m and 400m at the Atlanta Olympics

1967 **1991** **1992** **1996** **2000**

Wins gold in the 200m at the World Championships

Wins gold in the 400m and 4 x 400m relay at the Sydney Olympics

Sporting achievements

By the 1996 Atlanta Olympics, Johnson was the favourite to take the individual 400m and easily won the gold medal. Days later he won gold in the 200m, becoming the only male athlete to win gold in these two races at the same games. At the Sydney Olympics in 2000 Johnson won the 400m again. He crowned his Olympic career by winning gold for the USA in the 4 x 400m relay.

Did you know?

Johnson is famous for his gold-coloured running shoes.

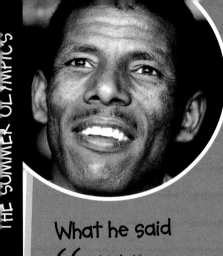

Haile Gebreselassie

Ethiopian long-distance runner Haile Gebreselassie won 10,000m gold at the 1996 Atlanta Olympics and the 2000 Sydney Olympics.

What he said

66 I think if you come first with a new world record, that is the best. 99

Did you know?

Gebreselassie set a world record for the marathon in 2007.

Find out more

Find out more about Gebreselassie at:
www.ethiopians.com/
haile_gebreselassie.htm

Find out more about Haile Gebreselassie at the official website of the Olympic movement:
www.olympic.org/uk/athletes/
index_uk.asp

Early life

Gebreselassie grew up in rural Ethiopia. He had to run 10 kilometres to school and back every day. Even today he runs with his left arm bent because for years he carried his school books with this arm.

Timeline

Born in Arsi, Ethiopia

Wins gold in the 10,000m at the Atlanta Olympics

Finishes fifth in the 10,000m at the Athens Olympics

1973   **1992**   **1996**   **2000**   **2004**   **2005**

Wins gold in the 5,000m at the World Junior Championships

Wins gold in the 10,000m at the Sydney Olympics

Wins the first of five marathons

Sporting achievements

Gebreselassie went to the 1996 Atlanta Games as the world record holder for 10,000m and the hot favourite to win the Olympic title. He lived up to expectations, but only just – he beat the Kenyan Paul Tergat by 6 metres to take the gold medal. Tergat and Gebreselassie fought another close contest at the Sydney Olympics in 2000. Tergat was ahead, but Gebreselassie overtook him with his last stride.

Kim Soo-Nyung

Kim Soo-Nyung competed for South Korea in individual and team **archery** events. She has won four gold medals at three Olympic Games.

Early life

Kim Soo-Nyung was just 17 years old when she won gold medals in both the individual and team archery events in front of a home crowd at the 1988 Seoul Olympics.

What they said

66 To South Korea, archery is like table tennis to China. 99

(Zhou Yuan, Chinese archery chief.)

Timeline

1971		1988	1991	1992		1999		2000

Wins individual and team gold medals at the Seoul Olympics

Wins individual silver and team gold at the Barcelona Olympics

Wins individual bronze and team gold at the Sydney Olympics

Born in Choong Chung Book Province, South Korea

Wins two gold medals at the World Championships

Starts training again after having two children

Did you know?

Arrows in archery competitions can travel as fast as 240 kilometres (149 miles) per hour.

Find out more

Find out more about archery at the official website of the Olympic movement: www.olympic.org/uk/sports/programme/index_uk.asp?SportCode=AR

Further achievements

Four years later, at the 1992 Barcelona Games, Kim Soo-Nyung won the individual silver medal and team gold. At the age of 21, she retired. Over the next seven years, Kim married and had two children. She returned to training in 1999 and qualified for the Sydney Games in 2000. This time she won bronze in the individual event and led her country to gold in the team event.

Cathy Freeman

Cathy Freeman was the first Australian **Aboriginal** athlete to win an Olympic medal. In 2000, she took the gold at the Sydney Games.

What she said

66 I was always surrounded by expectation from the very first race I ran as a 5 year-old. 99

Did you know?

Freeman's mother used to make her write "I am the world's greatest athlete" over and over again.

Early life

Freeman was born in Mackay, Queensland. She took part in her first race aged five. When she was 13, she told her teacher that she wanted to win a gold medal at the Olympic Games.

Timeline

1973	1994	1996	1997	2000	2003
Born in Queensland, Australia	Wins two gold medals at the Commonwealth Games	Wins silver in the 400m at the Atlanta Olympics	Wins gold in the 400m at the World Championships	Wins gold in the 400m at the Sydney Olympics	Retires from competition

Sporting achievements

Freeman was the first Aboriginal athlete to represent Australia at the 1996 Olympic games in Atlanta. She won silver in the 400m, coming second to the French athlete Marie-Jose Perec. When the 2000 Olympic Games were held in Sydney, Australia, everyone wanted to see Freeman win. She lit the Olympic flame at the opening ceremony and went on to fulfill expectations by winning the 400m gold in front of an ecstatic home crowd.

Jonathan Edwards

British athlete Jonathan Edwards was an outstanding triple jumper who took the gold medal at the 2000 Sydney Olympics.

Early life

Jonathan Edwards was an all-round athlete at school, but he went on to excel at the triple jump. By 1995, he had secured the world record in his event.

What he said

66 I couldn't believe I was in this stadium, at the Games and that I was the Olympic champion. 99

Timeline

Born in London, England

Wins silver at the Atlanta Olympics

Wins gold at the Commonwealth Games

| 1966 | 1995 | 1996 | 2000 | 2002 | 2003 |

Wins gold at the World Championships, setting a new world record

Wins gold at the Sydney Olympics

Retires from competition

Find out more

Find out more about Edwards at the BBC website: www.bbc.co.uk/pressoffice/ biographies/biogs/tvfactual/ jonathan_edwards.shtml

The British Olympians website has a profile of Jonathan Edwards: www.britisholympians.com/ athlete.aspx?at=1172

Sporting achievements

At the 1996 Olympics in Atlanta, Edwards jumped amazing distances. However, he fouled his longest jump and only took the silver medal. Edwards thought he had missed his chance at a gold medal, but he returned to compete at the 2000 Sydney Olympics. Finally, Edwards won gold with a jump of 17.71 metres in the third round.

Did you know?

Today, Edwards is a television sports presenter.

Sir Steven Redgrave

Sir Steven Redgrave is a British rower who won five gold medals at consecutive Olympic games.

What he said

66 Remember these six minutes for the rest of your lives. Listen to the crowd and take it all in. This is the stuff of dreams. 99

Did you know?

Since retiring from competitive rowing, Redgrave has run in three marathons.

Find out more

The official website of Redgrave:
www.steveredgrave.com

Find out more about rowing at the British Olympic website:
www.olympics.org.uk

Find out more about Redgrave at the official website of the Olympic movement:
www.olympic.org/uk/athletes/index_uk.asp

Early life

When Redgrave was at school, his teacher picked him to be a rower because he had big hands and feet. Despite suffering from illnesses, including diabetes, he made astonishing achievements in his rowing career.

Timeline

1962 Born in Marlow, England

1984 Wins gold in the **coxed** fours at the Los Angeles Games

1988 Wins gold in the **coxless** pairs at the Seoul Games and bronze in the coxed pairs

1992 Wins gold in the coxless pairs at the Barcelona Games

1996 Wins gold in the coxless pairs at the Atlanta Games

2000 Wins gold in the coxless pairs at the Sydney Games

2001 Redgrave is knighted

Sporting achievements

Redgrave won his first Olympic gold at the 1984 Los Angeles Games. He rowed as part of the British coxed fours crew. At the 1988 Seoul games, Redgrave won gold in the coxless pairs, as well as bronze in the coxed pairs. By the 1992 Barcelona Games, Redgrave was rowing with Matthew Pinsent, and they won the coxless pairs. They repeated the same feat in the 1996 Atlanta Games. In 2000, Redgrave went to Sydney looking for a fifth gold medal. He won with the coxless fours team.

Hicham El Guerrouj

Hicham El Guerrouj was a Moroccan **middle distance** runner who won gold in the 2004 Olympics in the 1,500m and 5,000m.

Early life

As a child, El Guerrouj saw his fellow Moroccan Said Aouita win the 5,000m at the 1984 Olympics. This inspired him to take up running himself.

What he said

❝It was tough but I tried to run easy. I have blisters from my shoes and I didn't sleep because of the joy I felt.❞

Timeline

1974	1996	1997	2000	2004	2006
Born in Berkane, Morocco		Wins the 1,500m at the World Championships for the first time		Wins gold in the 1,500m and 5,000m at the Athens Olympics	
	Trips and falls in the 1,500m at the Atlanta Olympics		Wins silver in the 1,500m at the Sydney Olympics	Retires from competition	

Did you know?

El Guerrouj is a UNICEF goodwill ambassador.

Find out more

Find out more about El Guerrouj at the official website of the Olympic movement: www.olympic.org/uk/athletes/index_uk.asp

Sporting achievements

El Guerrouj's first Olympic experience was bitterly disappointing. At the 1996 Atlanta Games, he tripped and fell in the 1,500m. Four years later at the Sydney Olympics, he was the favourite, but he was beaten by the Kenyan athlete Noah Ngeny and took the silver medal. At the 2004 Athens Olympics another Kenyan athlete, Bernard Lagat, threatened to win. El Guerrouj pulled ahead on the finishing line and took the gold medal. He followed up his success with a gold in the 5,000m.

Ian Thorpe

Australian swimmer Ian Thorpe won three gold medals at the Sydney Olympics in 2000 and two golds at the Athens Olympics four years later.

What he said

66 For myself, losing is not coming second. It's getting out of the water knowing you could have done better. 99

Did you know?

Thorpe was allergic to chlorine as a child, but he didn't stop swimming.

Early life

Thorpe started to swim when he was five. He was only 14 years old when he first represented Australia at the World Championships. He won gold in the 400m freestyle, becoming the youngest ever male world champion.

Timeline

Born in Sydney, Australia

1982

1998
Wins gold in the 400m freestyle and the 4 x 200m relay at the World Championships and four gold medals at the Commonwealth Games

Wins three gold medals and two silver medals at the Sydney Olympics

2000

2001
Wins six gold medals at the World Championships

Wins two gold medals, one silver, and one bronze at the Athens Olympics

2004

2006
Retires from competition

Sporting achievements

Thorpe was World Swimmer of the Year when he went to the Sydney Games in 2000. He had broken two world records just qualifying for the Australian Olympic squad. At the Sydney Games, Thorpe won gold medals in the 400m freestyle, the 4 x 100m, and 4 x 200m freestyle relays. He took another two silver medals and delighted the Australian crowd.

At the 2004 Athens Games, Thorpe took gold in the 400m and 200m freestyle, as well as bronze in the 100m freestyle and silver in the 4 x 200m relay.

Dame Kelly Holmes

Dame Kelly Holmes was a British middle-distance runner who took gold medals in the 800m and 1,500m at the 2004 Athens Olympics.

Early life

Holmes started competing as an athlete when she was 12 years old. When she was 13, she became the English Schools Athletics Champion. She joined the army but returned to athletics at the age of 22.

What she said

66 When you cross the line, it is such a wonderful feeling it's hard to describe. 99

Timeline

Born in Kent, England

Wins bronze in the 800m at the Sydney Olympics

Wins gold in the 800m and 1,500m at the Athens Olympics

1970   1994   2000   2002   2004   2005

Wins gold in the 1,500m at the Commonwealth Games

Wins gold in the 1,500m at the Commonwealth Games

Retires from competition

Find out more

The official website of Holmes: www.doublegold.co.uk

Find out more about Holmes at the official website of the Olympic movement: www.olympic.org/uk/athletes/index_uk.asp

Sporting achievements

Holmes won a bronze medal at the Sydney Olympics in 2000 but suffered injuries while she was training for the 2004 Games. She was fit by the time she arrived in Athens, planning only to run in the 1,500m. Five days before the 800m final she decided to run in that race, too. She won gold in both events, becoming the first British woman to win two Olympic gold medals in one competition.

Did you know?

Holmes was made a dame by the Queen in 2005.

Charles Jewtraw

American **speed skater** Charles Jewtraw won the first ever official Winter Olympics gold medal.

Sporting achievements

Jewtraw was an American speed skater. In 1924, Jewtraw went to Chamonix, France, to compete at the first ever Winter Olympics. He won gold in the 500m speed skating championship. This was the first ever Winter Olympics medal.

Find out more

Find out more about Jewtraw at the official website of the Olympic movement: www.olympic.org/uk/athletes/index_uk.asp

Timeline

National outdoor speed skating champion

Dies in Florida, USA

1900   **1921**   **1924**   **1996**

Born in New York, USA

Wins the gold medal for the 500m speed skating at the Chamonix Winter Olympics

Sonja Henie

Sonja Henie was a Norwegian figure skater who won three gold medals at the 1924 Winter Olympics in Chamonix, France.

Sporting achievements

Henie was only 11 years old when she took part in the first Winter Olympics in 1924. She won gold medals in **figure skating** at the Winter Olympics in 1928, 1932, and 1936.

Find out more

Find out about Henie and her skating achievements at: www.sonjahenie.net

Timeline

Born in Oslo, Norway

Wins World figure skating championships

Dies, aged 57

1912   **1924**   **1927**   **1928, 1932 & 1936**   **1969**

Goes to first Winter Olympics, aged 11

Wins gold medal in figure skating at three consecutive Olympics

Anton Sailer

Anton (Toni) Sailer was an Austrian skier who won three gold medals at the 1956 Winter Olympics.

Sporting achievements

Sailer was the first **alpine skier** to win the downhill, **slalom**, and giant slalom at the same Winter Olympics. Sailer achieved this extraordinary feat at the 1956 Winter Games in Cortina, Italy.

Timeline

Born in Kitzbühel, Austria — **1935**

1956 — Wins three gold medals at the Cortina Games

Retires from skiing — **1959**

1972 — Becomes chief trainer of the Austrian Skiing Association

Awarded the Olympic Order — **1985**

Find out more about Sailer at the official website of the Olympic movement: www.olympic.org/uk/athletes/index_uk.asp

Jean-Claude Killy

Jean-Claude Killy won three gold medals at the 1968 Winter Olympics in Grenoble, France.

Sporting achievements

Killy was a French skier who repeated Toni Sailer's triple gold medal win in the alpine skiing events at the 1968 Winter Olympics in Grenoble, France.

Find out more

Find out more about Killy at the official website of the Olympic movement: www.olympic.org/uk/athletes/index_uk.asp

Timeline

1943 — Born in Saint-Cloud, France

Wins skiing World Cup — **1967**

1968 — Wins three gold medals at Grenoble Winter Olympics

Stars in his first film — **1972**

1995 — Becomes a member of the International Olympic Committee

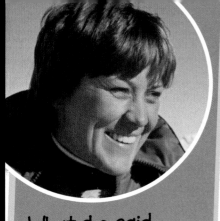

Rosi Mittermaier

West German skier Rosemarie Mittermaier took two gold medals and one silver medal at the 1976 Olympic Games in Innsbruck, Switzerland.

What she said

66 I don't feel like a heroine. You need luck. You have success when everything comes together in one day. 99

Did you know?

Downhill skiers can travel as fast as 136 kilometres (85 miles) per hour.

Find out more

Find out more about Mittermaier at the official website of the Olympic movement: www.olympic.org/uk/athletes/index_uk.asp

Find out more about alpine skiing at the official website of the Olympic movement: www.olympic.org/uk/sports

Early life

Mittermaier grew up in a skiing family in the Bavarian Alps. Her father ran a ski school, and her sister skied in the Winter Olympics of 1960 and 1964.

Timeline

Born in Bavaria, Germany

Takes part in Winter Olympics in Sapporo

1950   **1968**   **1972**   **1976**

Takes part in Winter Olympics in Grenoble

Wins two gold medals and one silver at the Winter Olympics in Innsbruck

Sporting achievements

Mittermaier had never won a downhill race in a major competition when she represented West Germany at the 1976 Olympic Games in Innsbruck. There, she won the Olympic gold medal in the downhill race by half a second. Three days later, she went on to win gold in the slalom. Expectations were high in the lead up to the giant slalom, as many people thought she would win a third gold medal. She skied an outstanding race but missed the gold medal by just 0.13 seconds, and took the silver medal. Her performance made her the most successful female Alpine skier in history at that time.

Eric Heiden

Eric Heiden was the first athlete to win five Olympic gold medals in individual events in the same games.

Early life

Heiden grew up in Wisconsin, USA. His parents enjoyed sport, and they encouraged their son to play ice hockey and football as a child. From the age of 14, Eric started to train as a speed skater.

What he said

66 Heck, gold medals, what can you do with them? 99

Timeline

1958	1976	1977	1980	1986	2002

Takes part in the 1,500m and 5,000m speed skating races at the Innsbruck Olympics (1976)

Wins five gold medals at the Lake Placid Winter Olympics (1980)

Joins the US Olympic speed skating team as a doctor (2002)

Born in Wisconsin, USA (1958)

Wins overall title at the World Championship (1977)

Cycles in the Tour de France (1986)

Did you know?

Heiden thought his greatest achievement was becoming a doctor, not an athlete.

Find out more

Find out about the sport of speed skating at:
www.usspeedskating.org

Find out more about Heiden at the official website of the Olympic movement:
www.olympic.org/uk/athletes/index_uk.asp

Sporting achievements

Heiden was just 17 years old when he took part in the 1976 Olympics in Innsbruck, Austria. In 1977, 1978, and 1979 he won the overall speed-skating title at the World Championships, so he went to the Lake Placid Games in 1980 as the hot favourite. He still surprized the world by winning all five Olympic speed skating events: 500m, 1,000m, 1,500m, 5,000m, and 10,000m. He also set a new Olympic record in every race.

Torvill and Dean

British figure skaters Jayne Torvill and Christopher Dean won Olympic gold at the 1984 Olympic Games in Sarajevo, in the former Yugoslavia.

What they said

❝ Tonight we reached the pinnacle. **❞**

(JT/CD.)

Did you know?

Torvill and Dean returned to the spotlight in 2006 on the television programme "Dancing on Ice".

Find out more

Find out more about figure skating at www.ice-dance.com

Find out more about Torvill and Dean at the official website of the Olympic movement. www.olympic.org/uk/athletes/index_uk.asp

Early life

Torvill started figure skating when she was eight years old. By the age of 14, she was National Pairs Champion. Dean began his skating career at the age of 10.

Timeline

| 1957 | 1958 | 1975 | 1981 | 1984 | 1994 | 1998 |

- Jayne Torvill born — 1957
- Christopher Dean born — 1958
- Torvill and Dean become skating partners — 1975
- They win figure skating World Championships for the first time — 1981
- Win gold at the Sarajevo Olympics — 1984
- Win bronze at the Lillehammer Olympics — 1994
- Retire from competition — 1998

Sporting achievements

Torvill and Dean came fifth in the ice-dancing competition at the 1980 Olympics. When they returned to the 1984 Olympics in Sarajevo they had already won gold four times at the World Figure Skating Championships. Their ice dance to Ravel's *Bolero* won them the gold medal. In 1994, they returned to the Olympics for a third time and took the bronze medal.

Matti Nykänen

Matti Nykänen is a Finnish ski jumper who won four Olympic gold medals during his career.

Early life

Nykänen was 12 years old when he made his first ski jump. By the age of 17, he was Finland's national champion. He became world champion two years later.

What he said

" When you're going for a jump, you're all by yourself. You have to make your own decisions yourself. "

Timeline

1963	1982	1984	1988	2008

Born in Jyväskylä, Finland

Takes gold and silver at the Sarajevo Olympics

Wins International Masters Championship

Wins his first gold medal in ski jumping at the World Championships

Wins three gold medals at the Calgary Olympics

Find out more

Find out more about Nykänen at the official website of the Olympic movement: www.olympic.org/uk/athletes/index_uk.asp

Find out more about ski jumping at the official website of the Olympic movement: www.olympic.org/uk/sports

Sporting achievements

At the 1984 Winter Olympics in Sarajevo in the former Yugoslavia, Nykänen won gold a nd silver medals in the ski jumping competition. He returned to defend his title at the 1988 Calgary Olympics in Canada and won gold in the normal hill event, the large hill event, and the large hill team competition. He was the first ski jumper to win three gold medals at the same Olympics.

Did you know?

After Nykänen retired from ski jumping he became a famous singer in Finland.

Janica Kostelić

Croatian alpine skier Janica Kostelić won four Olympic gold medals during her sporting career.

What she said

❝ I didn't really expect any of the medals, so I'm just really happy with what I have done. ❞

Did you know?

Kostelić's brother, Ivican, also won a silver medal at the 2006 Olympics.

Find out more

The official website of Kostelić: www.janica.hr

Find out more about Kostelić at the official website of the Olympic movement: www.olympic.org/uk/athletes/index_uk.asp

Early life

Kostelić started to ski when she was just three years old. When she was 13 she won an Olympic scholarship to help with her training.

Timeline

1982	1998	2001	2002	2006	2007
Born in Zagreb, Croatia	Takes part in the Nagano Olympics	Becomes World Cup Champion for the first time	Wins three golds and a silver medal at the Salt Lake City Olympics	Wins gold and silver at the Turin Olympics	Retires from competition

Sporting achievements

Kostelić was 16 years old when she took part in the 1988 Nagano Olympics in Japan. Despite suffering from injuries, Kostelić went to the 2002 Olympics in Salt Lake City and won gold medals in the slalom, giant slalom, and alpine combined events. She also won a silver medal and was the first female alpine skier to win four medals at one Olympics. In 2006, she added to her Olympic success with gold and silver medals at the Turin Games.

Rhona Martin

Rhona Martin was captain of the British women's **curling** team that won Olympic gold in 2002.

Early life

Martin first represented Scotland at junior level at the World Junior Championships in 1998.

What she said

"It's only because of the children that I went on. They were desperate for me to go to another Olympics."

Timeline

Born in Scotland

1966

Wins silver at the European Championships

1998

Wins gold at the Salt Lake City Olympics

2002

Comes fifth at the European Championships

2005

Takes part in Turin Olympics

2006

Did you know?

Curling was probably invented in medieval Scotland.

Sporting achievements

Martin had to deal with illness and competition from another Scottish team but eventually she qualified for the 2002 Olympics in Salt Lake City, USA. They won five out of their first seven matches, including two tie-break games, to get to the semi-finals. They had beaten Sweden, Germany, and Canada to reach the Olympic final, where they faced Switzerland. The competition was fierce, but Rhona led her team to a gold medal.

Find out more

Find out more about curling at the World Curling Federation's website: www.worldcurling.org

Find out more about curling at the official website of the Olympic movement: www.olympic.org/uk/sports

Arnold Boldt

Arnold (Arnie) Boldt is a Canadian single leg **amputee** who won gold medals in the high jump and long jump at the Paralympics.

What he said

66 I was fairly well accepted for who I was, it was quite easy to be yourself and do what you wanted to do without people pre-judging you. **99**

Did you know?

Boldt practised jumping on the family farm using bales of hay and sand pits.

Early life

Boldt lost his right leg in a farming accident when he was just three years old. He became involved in sport at primary school and was especially interested in high jump and standing long jump.

Timeline

1957	1976	1980	1984	1988	1992

Born in Manitoba, Canada

Wins gold medals in the high jump and the long jump at the Toronto Paralympics

Wins gold medal in the long jump and high jump at the Arnhem Paralympics

Wins gold medal in the high jump at the New York Paralympics

Wins gold in the high jump and silver in the long jump at the Seoul Paralympics

Wins gold in the high jump at the Barcelona Paralympics

Sporting achievements

Nineteen-year-old Boldt set world records and won gold medals in the high jump and long jump at the 1976 Toronto Paralympics in Canada. He was named "Outstanding Performer of the Games". At the 1980 Arnhem Paralympics in the Netherlands he repeated the double and broke his own world records in the process. Boldt went on to win gold in the high jump at three more Paralympic Games.

Mustapha Badid

The French athlete Mustapha Badid won five Paralympic gold medals in wheelchair racing.

Sporting achievements

At the 1984 New York Paralympics, Badid won gold in the 800m wheelchair race. At the Seoul Games in 1988 he swept the board with gold medals in the 200m, 1,500m, 5,000m, and marathon races.

Timeline

Wins one gold medal at the New York Paralympics

Wins the wheelchair division of the Boston marathon

1984   **1988**   **1990**

Wins four gold medals at the Seoul Paralympics

Find out more

Find out more about participating in sport with disabilities at the International Paralympic Committee's website:
www.paralympic.org

Trischa Zorn

Trischa Zorn is a visually impaired American swimmer. She has competed in every Paralympic Games from 1980 to 2004, winning a total of 55 medals.

Sporting achievements

Zorn began swimming at the age of seven. During her long career she won 41 gold, nine silver, and five bronze medals – more than any other Paralympic athlete.

Timeline

Born in California, USA

Wins 12 gold medals and sets nine world records at the Seoul Paralympics

1964   **1980**   **1988**   **2000**

Wins seven gold medals at the Arnhem Paralympics

Wins four silver and one bronze medal at the Sydney Paralympics

Find out more

Find out more information at the website for the International Blind Sport Federation:
www.ibsa.es/eng

Ajibola Adeoye

The Nigerian sprinter Ajibola Adeoye won the gold medal in the 100m at the 1992 Paralympics in Barcelona, Spain.

Sporting achievements

Adeoye has won five Paralympic medals but his greatest achievement came at the Barcelona Paralympics in 1992. He won the 100m for single-arm amputees a time that would have gained a fourth place in the Olympic games that year.

Find out more

Find out more about competing with a disability at the International Paralympic Committee's website: www.paralympic.org

Timeline

1992	1996
Wins gold medals in the 100m and 200m in Barcelona	Wins gold in the 100m and 200m and silver in the long jump

---

Ragnhild Myklebust

Norwegian skier Ragnhild Myklebust has won 22 Paralympic medals during her long sporting career.

Sporting achievements

The skier Myklebust competed in the **biathlon**, cross-country skiing, and ice-sledge racing events at the Paralympics. She has won the greatest number of Paralympic medals by one athlete. She was 58 years old when she won her last gold medal at the Salt Lake City Games in 2002.

Timeline

1988	1992	1994	1998
Wins five gold medals and one silver medal at the Innsbruck Games		Wins five gold, two silver, and two bronze medals at the Lillehammer Games	
	Wins two gold medals at the Tignes-Albertville Games		Wins five gold medals at the Nagano Games

Dame Tanni Grey-Thompson

British wheelchair racer Dame Tanni Grey-Thompson has won 16 Paralympic medals during her long sporting career.

Early life

Grey-Thompson was born with **spina bifida**. She enjoyed sports from an early age and tried wheelchair racing when she was 13.

What she said

66 It is about having a goal and a dream and doing everything you can to get there. 99

Timeline

Born in Cardiff, Wales

1969

Wins bronze in 400m at Seoul Paralympics

1988

Wins four gold medals in the 100, 200, 400, and 800m at the Barcelona Games and silver in the relay

1992

Wins the 800m gold and silver medals in the 100, 200, and 400m at the Atlanta Games

1996

Wins gold in the 100, 200, 400, and 800m at the Sydney Games

2000

Wins gold in the 100 and 400m at the Athens Games

2004

Find out more

The official website of Tanni Grey-Thompson: www.tanni.co.uk

Find out more about competing with a disability at the International Paralympic Committee's website: www.paralympic.org

Sporting achievements

Grey-Thompson's sporting career spanned nearly 20 years. She was 18 years old when she first represented Britain at wheelchair racing. She has dominated both the sprint and middle-distance events, winning four gold medals at both the Barcelona and Sydney Games. Overall she won 11 gold, four silver, and one bronze at Paralympics from 1988 to 2004.

Did you know?

Grey-Thompson has won the London marathon six times.

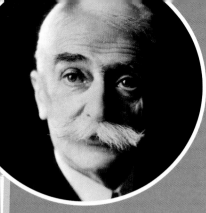

Pierre de Fredi

Pierre de Fredi, Baron de Coubertin, was the founder and the first secretary-general of the International Olympic Committee (IOC).

What he said

66 The important thing in life is not the victory but the contest; the essential thing is not to have won but to have fought well. 99

Did you know?

De Coubertin's heart is buried under a monument to him at Olympia in Greece.

Find out more

Find out lots more information on Pierre de Fredia and the founding of the International Olympic Committee at: www.olympic.org/uk/passion/museum/ permanent/index_uk.asp

Early life

Baron de Coubertin grew up in Paris and Normandy in France. His family was influential and wealthy and he was expected to join the military or go into politics. However, de Coubertin had a vision – to recreate the great sporting events of ancient Greece in the modern world.

Timeline

Born in Paris, France		Made President of the IOC		Dies in Geneva, Switzerland
1863	**1894**	**1896**	**1920**	**1937**
	Helps to found the IOC		Wins Nobel Peace Prize	

Achievements

In 1894, de Coubertin announced that he wanted to revive the Olympic Games, which had taken part in ancient Greece. He had seen Dr William Penny Brookes organize a version of the Olympic Games in London and wanted to take the idea and create an international competition. Later that year he founded the International Olympic Committee at a ceremony in Paris. He became President of the IOC in 1896 and at first struggled to spread enthusiasm for the games. However, by the 1906 Olympics in Paris, the games were recognized as the most important world sporting event. De Coubertin led the IOC until 1925.

Avery Brundage

Avery Brundage was President of the International Olympic Committee (IOC) at the 1972 Munich Games when 17 people were murdered in an attack by terrorists.

Early life

Brundage studied engineering at university but was also a strong all-round athlete. He took part in the 1912 Stockholm Olympics in Sweden and was all-round champion in the United States three times.

What he said

" We mourn our Israeli friends, victims of this brutal assault. The Olympic flag and the flags of all the world fly at half mast. "

Timeline

1887	1912	1936	1952	1972	1975
Born in Detroit, USA		Becomes a member of the IOC		Made Life Honorary President of the IOC	
	Takes part in the Stockholm Olympics		Becomes President of the IOC		Dies in West Germany

How did he die?

Brundage died three years after he retired as IOC president.

Find out more

Find out more about the terrorist attack during the Munich Games at: www.olympic.org/uk/games

Achievements

When Brundage retired from athletics, he became involved in the organization of sport. He was made President of the IOC in 1952. He was a controversial leader because he opposed women's participation in the Olympics and insisted on the amateur status of all competitors. Brundage is probably most famous for deciding to continue with the Munich Games in 1972 after Palestinian terrorists murdered 11 Israeli athletes. Most nations and athletes supported his decision.

Glossary

Aboriginal People who inhabited an area from earliest-known times.

alpine skier Person who competes in downhill skiing races, including slalom.

amputee Person who has had a limb or limbs removed.

appendicitis Disease of the appendix.

archery Shooting a bow and arrows.

athlete Person who takes part in sports.

biathlon Competition where athletes compete in two events.

boycott To refuse to take part in an event.

chariot Open carriage with two wheels that was pulled by horses in sport and in war.

Commonwealth Association of countries with historical links to Britain.

communist Form of government that believes all people should be equal.

coxed Rowing event where a person steers the boat.

coxless Rowing event with nobody steering the boat.

curling Game played by teams who slide discs on ice.

decathlon Competition where male athletes compete in ten events.

diaulos Race run at the ancient Olympics.

discus Throwing event where a dis- shaped plate is thrown.

field events Sporting events that include jumping and throwing.

figure skating Dancing on ice, either individually or in pairs.

freestyle Swimming stroke also known as front crawl.

heptathlon Competition where female athletes compete in eight events.

marathon Long-distance race of around 42 kilometres.

middle distance Running races such as the 5,000 metres or 10,000 metres.

Nazi Party Political party in Germany in the 1930s and 40s, led by Adolf Hitler.

pankration Mixture of boxing and wrestling in the ancient Olympics.

pentathlon Competition where athletes compete in five events.

polio Disease of the spine that can cause paralysis.

slalom Racing in and out of a line of posts in skiing.

Soviet Union Collection of states that were formerly part of Russia.

speed skating Racing on ice.

spina bifida Condition that affects the spine.

sprint Short race run at top speed.

stade Sprint race run at the ancient Olympics.

terrorist Person who uses the threat of or actual violence t achieve his or her aims.

triple jump Jumping event that used to be known as hop, step and jump.

Index

History and activities of

Ancient Greece

Greg Owens

www.heinemann.co.uk/library
Visit our website to find out more information about Heinemann Library books.

To order:
☎ Phone 44 (0) 1865 888066
  Send a fax to 44 (0) 1865 314091
📄 Visit the Heinemann Bookshop at www.heinemann.co.uk/library to browse our
💻 catalogue and order online.

First published in Great Britain by Heinemann
Library, Halley Court, Jordan Hill, Oxford OX2
8EJ, part of Harcourt Education. Heinemann is a
registered trademark of Harcourt Education Ltd.

© Harcourt Education Ltd 2007
The moral right of the proprietor has been
asserted.

Editorial: Audrey Stokes
Design: Kimberly R. Miracle in collaboration
with Cavedweller Studio
Picture research: Mica Brancic
Production: Camilla Crask

Origination: Chroma Graphics
Printed and bound in China by WKT
Company Limited

10-digit ISBN 0431080852
13-digit ISBN 9780431080857
11 10 09 08 07
10 9 8 7 6 5 4 3 2 1

British Library Cataloguing in Publication Data
Owens, Greg
Ancient Greece. – (Hands on ancient history)
1. Greece – Civilization – To 146 B.C. – Juvenile
literature
2. Greece – History – To 146 B.C. – Juvenile
literature
I. Title
938
A full catalogue record for this book is available
from the British Library.

Acknowledgements
The author and publishers are grateful to
the following for permission to reproduce
photographs: Ancient Art and Architecture
Collection, pp. 7, 8, 18 (C M.Dixon), 26; Art
Directors and Trip, p. 20 (Helene Rogers);
Bridgeman Art Library, pp. 6 (Museo
Archeologico Nazionale, Naples, Italy), 14;
Corbis, pp. 11 (Araldo de Luca), 13 (Elio Ciol),
15 (Bettmann), 16 (Michael Nicholson), 17
(Yiorgos Karahalis/Reuters), 22 (Araldo de
Luca); Harcourt, pp. 19 (David Rigg), 25 (David
Rigg), 29 (David Rigg); NorthWind Pictures, p.
9; Photo Scala, Florence, p.12 (Courtesy of the
Ministero Beni e Att. Culturali).

Cover photographs of an ancient Greek vase
(foreground) reproduced with permission of
Getty Images/ Bridgeman Art Library and
Parthenon (background) reproduced with
permission of Getty Images/ Photodisc.

The publishers would like to thank Greg Aldrete,
Eric Utech and Kathy Peltan for their assistance
in the preparation of this book.

Every effort has been made to contact copyright
holders of any material reproduced in this book.
Any omissions will be rectified in subsequent
printings if notice is given to the publishers.

Contents

Some words are shown in bold, **like this.** You can find out what they mean by looking in the glossary.

Chapter 1: The world's first democracy

Greece is a country in southern Europe. It includes many small islands in the Mediterranean Sea. The first **civilization** in this area was the Minoans. They lived on the island of Crete. Many of their cities were destroyed in about 1450 BCE. Some scientists think that a volcano was to blame. Soon other cultures developed in Greece.

Ancient Greece was made up of many smaller settlements. Some were on the mainland and others were on islands. Mountains or water often separated these communities. Each small community was known as a city-state, or *polis*. Each city-state had its own laws. The city-states often fought with each other. Sometimes they banded together to fight outside forces. The most famous city-states were Athens and Sparta.

The ancient Greeks gave us many beliefs and ideas. One of the most important ideas was about government. Before the Greeks, most people were ruled by kings or small groups who held power over everyone. The Greeks created something new: a government where people had rights. In Greek society, people created their own laws. It was called **democracy**.

Timeline

1600–1100 BCE
Mycenaean civilization

479 BCE Greeks defeat invading Persians, ending the Persian Wars

338 BCE King Philip II of Macedon conquers Greece

2800–1450 BCE
Minoan civilization based on the island of Crete

750–490 BCE
Rise of independent Greek city-states and self-government

404 BCE
Athens falls to Sparta, ending Peloponnesian Wars

146 BCE
Greece becomes part of the Roman Empire

The phrase BCE means "Before the Common Era", a time before Christianity was a popular religion. The term BC is also used to mean the same thing.

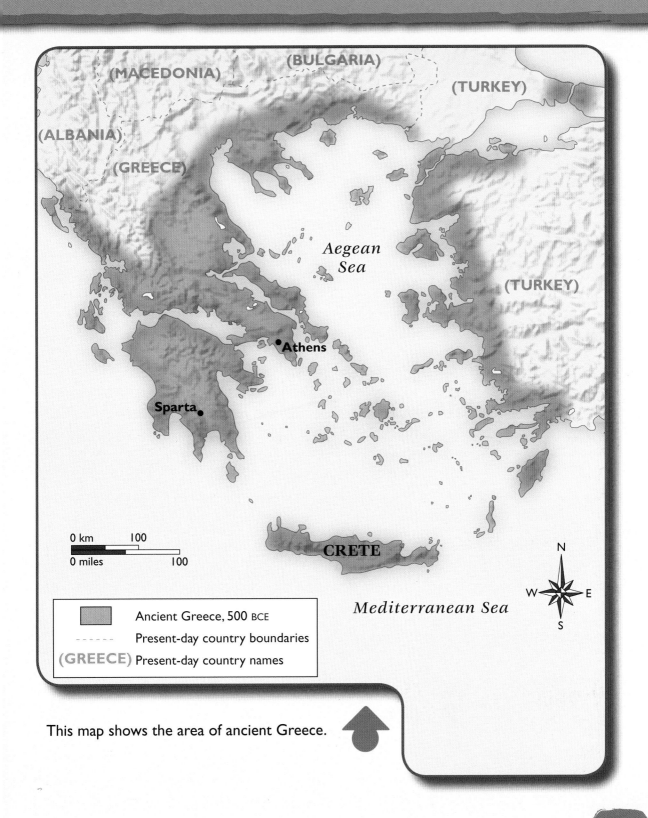

(MACEDONIA)

(BULGARIA)

(TURKEY)

(ALBANIA)

(GREECE)

Aegean
Sea

(TURKEY)

●Athens

Sparta●

0 km   100

0 miles   100

CRETE

Mediterranean Sea

N
W   E
S

Ancient Greece, 500 BCE

Present-day country boundaries

(GREECE) Present-day country names

This map shows the area of ancient Greece.

Athens and Sparta were both city-states, but they were very different. The people of Athens were proud of their culture and knowledge. Spartans thought that strength and military power were most important.

Athens

Until 508 BCE, kings and rich landowners controlled Athens. There were strict rules about who could own land. A person who owed money could be forced to work as a slave. In 508, a leader named Solon passed new laws to change those rules. These changes made the government more democratic. The word **"democracy"** comes from two ancient Greek words – *"demos"* meaning "people" and *"kratia"* meaning "power". So, democracy means "people power".

Athens was divided into ten tribes. Fifty men from each tribe formed a group called the Council. The Council made all the laws. These laws had to be approved by the Assembly. The Assembly included all male **citizens** of Athens.

 Solon was the leader who brought democracy to ancient Greece.

6

The *bouleterion* was the original meeting place of the Athenian council.

In court, any citizen could bring charges against another. Both the accuser and the accused spoke for themselves. There were no lawyers. The jury voted using circular tokens. A token with a hollow centre meant guilty. A token with a solid centre meant innocent.

A democracy did not mean that everyone was free. Women, slaves, and non-citizens had few rights. But it was the first time in history that people had the right to determine their own government.

The beginning of democracy

"The many were in slavery to the few, the people rose against the upper class. The strife was keen, and for a long time the two parties were ranged in hostile camps against one another, till at last, by common consent, they appointed Solon to be mediator and Archon (leader), and committed the whole **constitution** to his hands."

From *The Athenian Constitution* by Aristotle, written 350 BCE.

7

Sparta

Sparta was ruled by an **oligarchy**. This meant a few powerful people controlled everything. Spartan culture was based around the military. Boys began training to be soldiers at the age of seven. They began active duty at twenty and continued as soldiers until they turned 60.

The Spartans believed in dressing, eating, and living very simply. Today we still use the word "spartan" to mean bare or plain. In Athens, the individual was most important. In Sparta, the individual was less important than the state.

There were slaves in Sparta called *helots*. They mostly worked on the farms that were given to the soldiers by the state. Even though Sparta was less democratic than Athens, women in Sparta owned property and had more rights.

This statue shows a soldier wearing a Spartan military helmet.

War between Athens and Sparta

Athens and Sparta were the two most powerful city-states in the ancient Greek world. Although they fought together against foreign invaders, they remained enemies. Each tried to influence other city-states to live like them.

In 431 BCE, Athens and Sparta began a series of battles that lasted almost 30 years. This was known as the Peloponnesian War. When the war was over, Sparta conquered Athens and set up an oligarchic government. It was known as the Thirty Tyrants. Greek **democracy** survived a little bit in different city-states. But it was never as strong as it had been in Athens before the war.

This picture shows daily life in Sparta.

Chapter 2: Life in ancient Greece

Most Greek houses were built with bricks. The bricks were made from mud that had been dried in the sun. The house was a big square with an open courtyard in the centre. The courtyard often had a well or a tank for the family's water supply. The walls of these homes were sometimes decorated with a type of painting known as fresco.

The Greek home was divided into the male area (*andron*) and the female area (*gunaikon*). Women did all the cooking and household chores, so the kitchen was part of the *gunaikon*. The *andron* was a room with several long couches. This was where men and their male friends enjoyed their time away from work or business.

Food and clothing

This illustration shows a typical ancient Greek home.

Oikos

The Greek word for house is *oikos*. From this came the word *oikonomia*, which means "household management". This is where the modern English word "economy" comes from. The word "ecology", which refers to the study of living things and their environments, also comes from *oikos*.

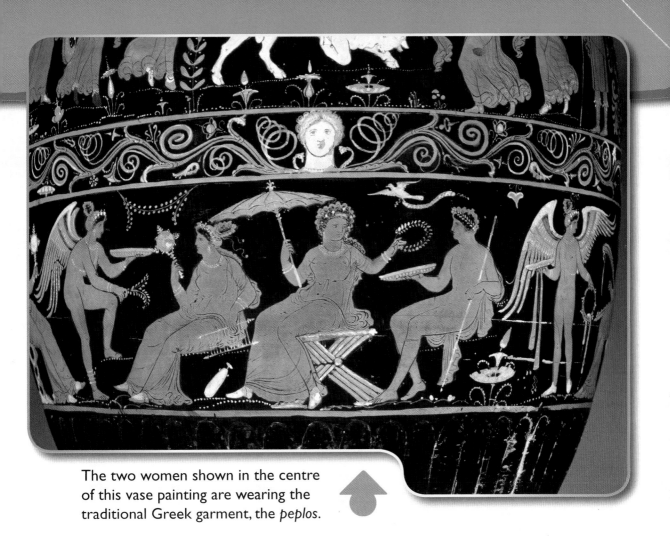

The two women shown in the centre of this vase painting are wearing the traditional Greek garment, the *peplos*.

The main piece of clothing worn by both women and men was a large rectangular piece of wool. It was wrapped around the body, then pinned at the shoulder and tied at the waist. For men, this garment was called a *chiton*. For women, it was called a *peplos*.

Wheat, wine, and olive oil were three main parts of the ancient Greek diet. People also ate grapes, figs, and sesame seeds. They had vegetables such as beans and peas. In the coastal areas they ate a lot of fish. Many ancient Greeks kept goats and either drank their milk or made cheese from it. They did not eat very much meat.

Children

Greek children were wrapped up tightly in blankets and carried around until they were almost three years old. They spent most of their time with their mothers. When they were old enough to run and play, they often played in the outdoor courtyard of their house.

One of the most popular games was called knucklebones. It was played by tossing small bones up in the air. Then you had to catch them on the back of your hand. Ancient Greek children also played with yo-yos and dolls. They had other toys made from terracotta pottery.

 This terracotta statue shows young people playing a game of knucklebones. It is from about 300 BCE.

There was no law in ancient Greece that said children had to go to school. Most boys were sent to school by the time they were seven years old. There were few schools for girls because parents believed girls should stay at home to learn to run the household. Most children went to school for three or four years and at least learned to read. Pupils from wealthier families went to school for up to ten years.

School was divided into three main categories. The first included the study of reading, writing, arithmetic, and literature. The second category was athletics. Wrestling, gymnastics, and other athletic activities were part of the school curriculum. Music was the third category. Students were taught to sing and play a stringed instrument called a lyre.

"Alphabet"

In 403 BCE, Athens adopted the official form of the 24-letter Greek alphabet. The English word "alphabet" comes from the first two letters of the ancient Greek alphabet – alpha and beta.

The Greek alphabet, shown here, has 24 letters.

The *agora*, or marketplace, in Athens was the original meeting place of the Council, and also where people gathered to meet or shop.

Work

Most ancient Greeks were farmers. They grew olives and wheat and made wine. They raised sheep and goats on dry, rocky land that got little rain.

Trade was important to the Greek city-states. The merchants who traded were a major group of Greek workers. Sailors who carried goods back and forth across the ocean were another important group of workers. There were also doctors, architects, bankers, fishermen, carpenters, athletes, teachers, musicians, and actors.

Up to half of the people in Athens at this time were slaves. Most slaves were people from other countries. Many were captured during wars and forced into slavery. They did everything from household chores to dangerous work in silver mines.

Religion

The ancient Greeks believed in twelve main gods and goddesses who lived on Mount Olympus. The Greeks had a set of myths, or stories, from the distant past. These explained the origins and history of their people and their world. The Greeks built many temples and made offerings and animal sacrifices. They hoped to get the gods to help them. Now when we study these stories of the ancient Greek religion, we often refer to it as **mythology**.

Olympian gods and goddesses

Zeus – king of the gods
Poseidon – god of the sea
Hades – king of the dead
Hestia – goddess of the hearth, or home
Hera – goddess of marriage, Zeus' queen
Ares – god of war
Athena – goddess of wisdom
Apollo – god of music and healing
Aphrodite – goddess of love and beauty
Hermes – the messenger god
Artemis – goddess of the hunt
Hephaestus – god of fire

Zeus was the king of the Olympian gods.

Chapter 3: Arts and sports

The ancient Greeks thought that **intellectual** and physical activities were both very important. They were the first people to put on plays in a theatre. The ancient Greeks also invented the Olympics.

Greek theatre

Every year, Athens hosted a religious celebration that lasted for several days. Thousands of people would gather in the Theatre of Dionysus. They watched plays based on Greek myths. These plays were huge productions. They often included dozens of actors, dancers, and musicians.

The Greeks invented a type of play known as "tragedy", which did not have a happy ending. The ancient Greek word *"tragoedia"* meant "goat song". They either called it tragedy because the actors wore goat skins, or because a goat was sacrificed before the show.

The Theatre of Dionysus hosted the great dramatic festivals of ancient Greece.

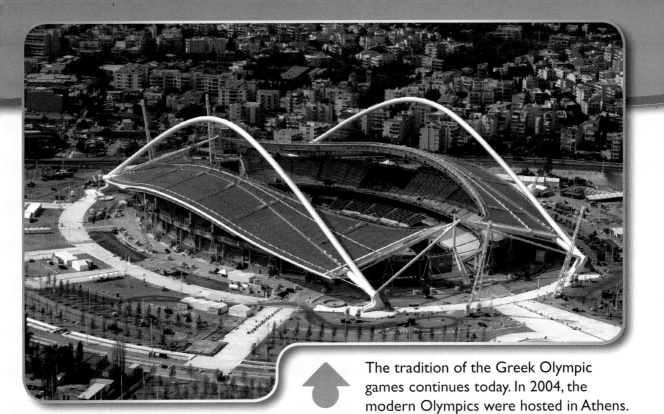

The tradition of the Greek Olympic games continues today. In 2004, the modern Olympics were hosted in Athens.

The Olympics

In 776 BCE, the ancient Greeks held the first athletic competition at Olympia, an area sacred to the god Zeus. They started having these competitions every four years. Men from all over Greece competed for the honour of their city-states. There was an olive crown that went to the winner.

At first, the ancient Olympics was just a one-day running event. It later developed into a five-day competition in running, jumping, wrestling, and javelin throwing.

Heraea games

The ancient Greeks did not allow women to compete in Olympic events. Married women were not even allowed to attend the Olympics. But there was an athletic competition just for women known as the Heraea Games. It was named after the goddess Hera, wife of Zeus. This competition happened every five years. Women competed in running and chariot races, as well as drama and music.

By doing the recipe and activities in this chapter you will get an idea of what life was like for people living in ancient Greece.

Recipe: sesame buns

Sesame seeds were one of the earliest food sources of the ancient world. Records of its use date back at least 4,000 years. The sesame plant was used for food, spice, oil, and even ink by ancient cultures in Assyria, China, and Egypt. In ancient Greece, soldiers ate sesame seeds as an energy food. Sesame seeds with honey were also served at ancient Greek festivals and weddings.

Warning!

An adult should always be present when you are cooking.

Make sure you read all directions before beginning the recipe.

Supplies
- 500 g whole wheat flour
- 250 ml of milk
- 125 ml of olive oil
- 3 eggs
- 1 teaspoon of crushed aniseed
- 1 teaspoon of salt
- 200 g of sesame seeds
- 250 ml of honey
- greased baking tray

People of ancient Greece enjoy a banquet in this scene from a vase painting.

1. Preheat the oven to 180 °C (356 °F)

2. Mix the salt and the crushed aniseed with the flour and add the olive oil and the eggs while you knead the mixture.

3. Add the milk, half of the honey, and half of the sesame seeds to the flour mixture.

4. Form the flour mixture into bun shapes and put them on a greased baking tray.

5. Make a small hole in the middle of each bun. Fill these holes with the rest of the honey and sprinkle them with the rest of the sesame seeds.

6. Bake for 40 minutes, or until they are golden brown.

Sesame buns

With a few simple ingredients, you can make these tasty sesame buns in about an hour.

Activity: Make a *peplos*

The primary piece of clothing for ancient Greek men and women was the *chiton*. It is often confused with the Roman toga, but it is different. The ancient Greeks mostly wore *chitons* made of wool. A *chiton* was worn long by women, short by children, and either long or short by men.

It is basically a tube of fabric slipped over the head, and suspended on the shoulders. A belt could be worn around the waist. The women's *chiton* was called a *peplos*. You can make your own out of a simple piece of cloth.

Supplies
- single bedsheet or similar-sized fabric
- safety pins
- belt, sash, or rope
- fabric glue or sewing materials (optional)
- fabric paint or markers (optional)
- Greek-style ribbon or binding (optional)

A

❶ Fold the fabric in half. Reach your arms out side-to-side. Ask a friend to make sure the fabric is wide enough to reach from one of your elbows to the other. Also make sure it reaches from your forehead to your knees or ankles, depending on how long you want it to be. (See Picture A)

❷ Fasten the fabric closed along the long edge to form a large cloth tube. An adult can help you sew the long edge closed, or use fabric glue or safety pins to close the edge. You can even leave the edge open and use the belt to keep it closed later.

3 If you have closed the long edge of the tube, turn it inside-out so the sewing or pins do not show. Slip the tube over your head so the top edge is just below your armpits. (See picture B)

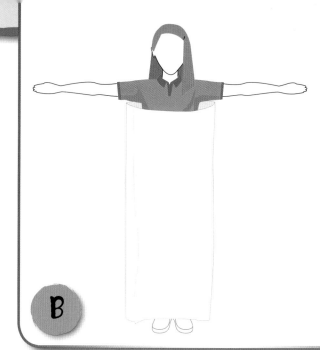

B

C

4 Ask a friend to help you bunch the fabric so that you can pull the front and back of it over each shoulder. Secure with large safety pins. These are the straps that hold the *peplos* onto your shoulders. (See Picture C)

5 Tie a belt, sash, or rope around your waist to hold the fabric in place and keep you comfortable. (See Picture D)

6 Now that you know how to wear your *peplos*, you could decorate the edges with a typical Greek pattern. You can use markers or paint to decorate it, or sew or glue ribbon or binding onto the *peplos*.

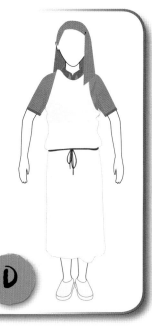

D

◀ *Peplos*

This illustration shows what your ancient Greek *peplos* will look like when it is finished.

How would your wardrobe change if you had to make all of your own clothes?

Activity: make a Greek vase

One of the crafts for which the ancient Greeks are best known is their vase painting. There were two main kinds of vase painting. Black figure vases showed people or objects in black against a red background. Red figure vases were just the opposite. This activity will show you how to make your own painted Greek vase.

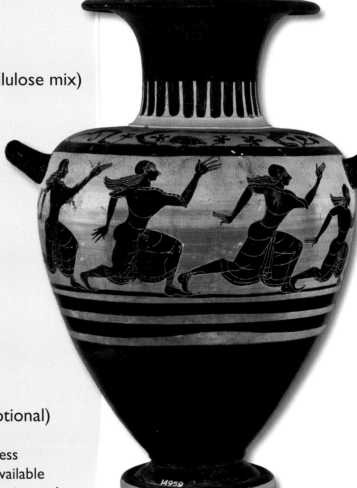

Warning!

This project is messy. A washable work surface and an overall are recommended.

Make sure you read all of the directions before beginning the project.

Supplies

- newspaper and/or white paper towels
- masking tape
- papier-mâché paste (high-cellulose mix)
- large bowl for making papier-mâché
- balloon
- cardboard tube: toilet tissue roll size for small balloon, large wrapping paper roll size for larger balloon
- thick cardboard cut into disc, larger in diameter than the cardboard roll
- pencil
- drawing paper
- paint and brush
- non-toxic acrylic varnish (optional)

Note: For a stronger vase with less drying time, use plaster gauze (available from craft shops) dipped in water instead of the newspaper strips and papier-mâché.

This ancient Greek vase painting shows a group of women running.

1. Inflate the balloon and tie it closed.

2. Cut off about 5 centimetres of the cardboard tube. Tape this piece securely to one end of the balloon. Repeat this process, cutting another, longer piece of tube and taping it to the other end of the balloon. Tape the cardboard disc to one of the tubes. This will be the base of your vase. (See Picture A)

A

B

3. Roll a page of newspaper into a tube. Take the ends of the tube and twist the newspaper so it is like a coiled rope. Use tape to connect one end of the newspaper to the side of the balloon, and connect the other end to the cardboard tube on the top of your balloon. This is one of the handles. Repeat this process to make a second handle so both sides of the jar match. (See Picture B)

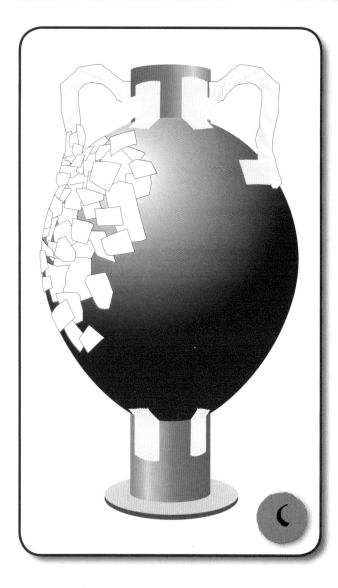

4 Make sure that everything is taped securely.

5 In a large bowl, mix the papier-mâché paste, according to the package directions.

6 Tear the newspaper into 2.5 centimetre-strips. Dip the newspaper into the paste, covering both sides. Pull the newspaper through your fingers to remove the excess papier-mâché. Carefully lay the strip onto the balloon, starting at the base and working your way up to the top. Extend it over the masking tape and cardboard pieces. Continue dipping and placing strips onto the balloon, covering it and the cardboard and the handles with an even layer. (See Picture C)

7 Cover the entire vase at least three times with papier-mâché. When you reach your last layer, you could use strips of paper towels instead of newspaper, so that your vase is white and easy to paint when it dries. Use a pencil to write your name on a piece of paper towel and paste it onto the balloon so you know which vase is yours when it dries overnight.

8 When the vase is dry paint it white (unless it is white already).

9 On a piece of drawing paper, sketch your ideas for the vase's decoration.

10 Use your pencil to draw your design on the vase. Paint your design carefully. When it dries you can make the paint shiny by covering it with acrylic varnish or white glue.

◀ Greek vase

This is what a home-made painted vase looks like when it is finished.

You could show an athlete, or heroic person, or character from Greek mythology. What are some modern ideas you might choose for a design?

Activity: make a fresco painting

Fresco is a type of painting style that was invented by the ancient Greeks. These paintings were done on plaster walls while the plaster was still wet. This made the colours of the painting very bright. The ancient Greeks painted frescoes on the walls of their temples and houses for decoration.

Supplies

- cardboard box
- pencil and paper
- ruler
- clear sticky tape
- cutting mat
- craft knife
- newspaper
- thick cord, string, or rope
- paint
- plaster
- poster paints
- paint brushes
- container for mixing plaster

Fresco painting was invented by the ancient Greeks. This fresco shows a warrior and his horse.

1 Draw a design for your fresco.

2 When you are happy with your design, use the cardboard to make a mould the same size. The sides should be five centimetres deep. Ask an adult to score the sides with the craft knife and turn them up. Tape the sides together to form a box. (See Picture A)

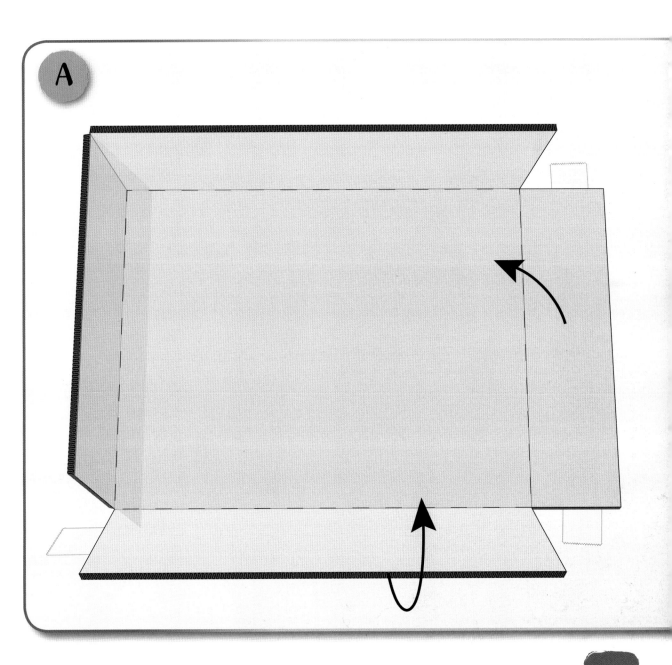

A

B

3 Follow the directions on the container of plaster for mixing it. Then pour the mixed plaster into your mould to a depth of three centimetres. (See Picture B)

4 Smooth the surface of the plaster. Remember that you will be drawing on the plaster so it should be as smooth as possible. Before the plaster dries, cut some cord or string into a piece that is fifteen centimetres long. Push the ends into the top of the wet plaster. This creates a loop to hang the fresco by when it is dry. (See Picture C)

5 When the plaster is dry, carefully remove it from the mould. Use a pencil to draw your design on the smooth surface of the plaster.

6 Use the poster paints to paint your design.

What kinds of designs would be appropriate in your house? What about in a Greek house?

Fresco

This fresco painting was made using the instructions on the previous pages.

Glossary

citizen person who lives in a town or city

civilization literature, traditions, customs, religion, and physical structures of a particular people at a particular place in time

constitution written record of the set of laws that govern a state or country

democracy system of government in which all people have the power to decide how they will live

mythology study of the myths, or stories, that different cultures tell to explain their origins and the world around them

oligarchy system of government in which a few powerful individuals control everything

More books to read

Arts and Crafts of the Ancient World: *Ancient Greece*, Ting Morris (Watts Publishing, 2006)

Excavating the Past: Ancient Greece, Christine Hatt (Heinemann Library, 2004)

Understanding People in the Past: the Ancient Greeks, Rosemary Rees (Heinemann Library, 2006)

You are in Ancient Greece, Ivan Minnis (Raintree Perspectives, 2004)

The instructions for the crafts and activities are designed to allow pupils to work as independently as possible. However, it is always a good idea to make a prototype before assigning any project so that pupils can see how their own work will look when completed. Prior to introducing these activities, teachers should collect and prepare the materials and be ready for any modifications that may be necessary. Participating in the project-making process will help teachers understand the directions and be ready to assist pupils with difficult steps. Teachers might also choose to adapt or modify the projects to better suit the needs of an individual child or class. No one knows the levels of achievement pupils will reach better than their teacher.

While it is preferable for pupils to work as independently as possible, there is some flexibility in regards to project materials and tools. They can vary according to what is available. For instance, while standard white glue may be most familiar, there might be times when a teacher will choose to speed up a project by using a hot glue gun to join materials. Where plaster gauze is not availabe, papier mâché can often be used. Likewise, while a project may call for leather cord, in most instances it is possible to substitute plastic rope or even wool or string. Acrylic paint may be recommended because it adheres better to a material like felt or plastic, but other types of paint would be suitable as well. Circles can be drawn with a compass, or simply by tracing a cup, roll of tape, or other circular object. Allowing pupils a broad spectrum of creativity and opportunities to problem-solve within the parameters of a given project will encourage their critical thinking skills most fully.

Each project contains a question within the directions. These questions are meant to be thought-provoking and promote discussion while pupils work on the project.

Index

Titles in the *Hands on Ancient History* series include:

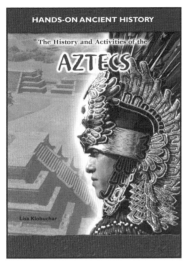

Hardback   978 0 431 08083 3

Hardback   978 0 431 08086 4

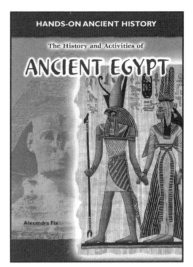

Hardback   978 0 431 08084 0

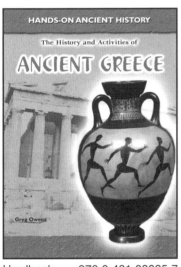

Hardback   978 0 431 08085 7

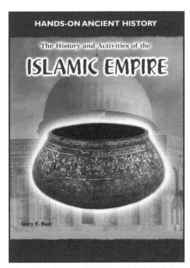

Hardback   978 0 431 08089 5

Hardback   978 0 431 08087 1

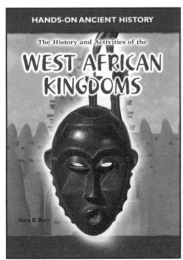

Hardback   978 0 431 08088 8

Find out about other titles from Heinemann Library on our website www.heinemann.co.uk/library